Heading Out

Though we sailed outside when the sun rode high,
When night came on we sought the lee,
Finding sweet sleep,
Like the homing birds,
Up the long curve flowing down to the sea.

HEADING OUT

*Selected Poems
by Virginia Linton*

WILLIAM L. BAUHAN PUBLISHER
DUBLIN, NEW HAMPSHIRE

COPYRIGHT © 1981 BY VIRGINIA LINTON

All rights reserved. No portion of this book may be reproduced without permission of the publisher except by reviewers quoting brief passages in newspapers or periodicals.

Library of Congress Cataloguing in Publication data:
Linton, Virginia, 1913–
  Heading Out
  I. Title.
PS3562.I555H4   811'.54   80-23182
ISBN O-87233-054-0

ILLUSTRATIONS BY JULIA DAUGETTE

PRINTED IN THE UNITED STATES OF AMERICA

For W.R.L. with love

Acknowledgments

The author expresses her thanks to the following publications for permission to reprint some of the poems appearing in this volume:
Bay Leaves: The Interior. *Chatelaine*: Night Swim in September. *Chicago Tribune Magazine*: The Cold Sky. *Christian Science Monitor*: Over the Bounding May. *The Island Packet*: The Sailing Party, Here, A Sometime Thing. *Islander*: Close by the Mangrove Meadows, Autumn Marsh: Updated, Where the Tree Grows Green, The Community of Snakes, Crab's Path, Birdwatcher's Winter Beach. *The Ladies Home Journal:* Lines to a Young Ballerina. *The London Daily Telegraph Magazine*: The Sailing Party, Differing Views of a Dead Whale, A Sometime Thing, When the House Pinches, The Fifty Dogs of Bimini, Doldrums, Mischief, Where the Tree Grows Green, Early Breakfast, Sticks and Stones are Feathers, The Cold Sky. *The New York Times*: Doldrums, The Ramblers. *The Poetry Society of American Bulletin*: The Sense of an Alien Presence. *Poetry Society of Georgia Yearbook*: Crab's Path, Autumn Marsh: Updated, The Clearest Image, When I Consider the Beneficence of Unpolluted Air, Close by the Mangrove Meadows, On Having Arrived at the Timber Line, Here. *The South Carolina Review*: Differing Views of a Dead Whale, Hidden Image. *Southern World Magazine*: Two Songs, Above the Monarch's Wing, Doldrums.

The New York Times Book of Verse: The Ramblers. *The Poetry Society of America Diamond Anthology*: Close by the Mangrove Meadows. *Poetry Society of Georgia Anthology of Verse*: Close by the Mangrove Meadows, Crab's Path. *People Within*: (Thornhill Press, Gloucester, England) Differing Views of a Dead Whale.

Differing Views of a Dead Whale won a Guinness Award (England, 1972). *The Sense of an Alien Presence* won the Emily Dickinson Award of the Poetry Society of America in 1979.

Contents

1 • POEMS OF PASSAGE

11   The Sailing Party
13   The Undertow
14   *Great God, I'd Rather be a Pagan . . .*
15   Close by the Mangrove Meadows
16   Differing Views of a Dead Whale
17   *So is This Great and Wide Sea . . .*
18   Caught by an Eye
19   Here
21   Heading Out
22   This Sea (Early)
23   This Sea (Late)
24   *About the Pleasures Known to Fishermen . . .*
25   A Sometime Thing
27   *From Proust's Contre Sainte Beauve*
28   Daytime Moon Overhead
29   After the Quarrel
30   *Hermit Crab — Webster*
31   When the House Pinches
32   The Fifty Dogs of Bimini
33   Doldrums
34   Voyage to Nowhere
35   *DuBartas: But for Chaste Love . . .*
36   School of Mullet
37   Birdwatcher's Winter Beach
38   Night Swim in September
39   Crab's Path
40   Which Swim do you Want

[7]

II • THE ARROGANT FLOWER

43 Beside the Castalia Fountain
44 Mischief
45 Where the Tree Grows Green
46 Sticks and Stones are Feathers
47 The Community of Snakes
48 *Darwin: The Beauty of a Flower*
49 The Clearest Image
50 When I Consider the Beneficence of Unpolluted Air
51 The Sense of an Alien Presence
52 The Cold Sky
53 Lines to a Young Ballerina
54 The Last Visit
55 *Poetry Cannot be Taught . . .*
56 The Papal Audience
57 *At Serengeti*
58 The Interior
60 Two Songs
61 On Having Arrived at the Timber Line
62 Harsanyi
63 *Shelley: A Man Cannot Say "I will compose poetry."*
64 Pas De Trois
65 Hidden Image
66 Early Breakfast
67 The Earth Does not Always Move Twice
68 The Ramblers
69 Above the Monarch's Wing
70 *The Swallow*
71 Over the Bounding May
72 Prelude
73 Autumn Marsh: Updated
74 Looking Alive at Jacob's Pillow
75 Son
76 Treading the Gentle Water
78 The X-Ray

I • Poems of Passage

The Sailing Party

The world spun blue and white that day,
The blue, beyond the mind's credulity;
The houses rising by the shore,
And the men who waded to their thighs,
All but leapt with clarity
As we sailed by,
Through the short, hard chop of the inlet
To the long flow and swell of the sea.

The change came almost imperceptibly,
As combers, rising green,
With a hard glass sheen,
And a soft hiss at their lips,
Began to boom—
Each with a tall soaring roar—
On the beach,
Beyond sight, beyond call, beyond reach.

One caught us on our beam; and rising,
Hove us canted toward the sky;
Then, in silence, brief and pale—
We had no breath to scream—
We hung in the curl
Of that cold foaming lip,
Like a shell,
While the mast brushed the trough of the wave.

We trimmed ship. And we bailed. Then we
Came running in, the seas lunging
High at our stern. Shouting

And laughing, we rode the combers
As they came—which was odd, knowing
The combers, had luck failed,
Would have raced and hissed their way
All day, as though
We five had neither died nor been—

But only emerged, again and again,
Before turning—singing the wind still—
Back to the sea.

The Undertow

There was always
that *cat's paw*
in his mind   ready

to snatch him (grinding
his face
into sea-floor grit
and gelatinous gunk)

over the reef.

Finding it worst
in the shallows,
he learned—eyeing

spindrift
and the glisten of crests—

to swim for the deeps.

*Great God,
I'd rather be a pagan,
Suckled in a creed outworn,
So might I, standing on this pleasant lea,
Have glimpse of Triton rising from the sea,
And hear old Proteus blow his wreathed Horn.*

—William Wordsworth

A variation of gulls hovered: canted
and swung closer, on an indiffrent air,
mewling together their feather-light blanket—
deceiving soft as grey cloud-cover—

Calling in,
up the long sea-wind, a congregation of celebrants.

So is *this great and wide sea,*
wherein are *things creeping innumerable,*
both small and great beasts.

There go the ships: there is *that*
leviathan, whom *thou hast made*
to play therein.

—Psalm 104, Verses 25 and 26

Caught by an Eye

one
cruising pelican

his slack pouch
stretching
like a thin

black rubber bag

to let the mullet
bump
        lumpy
              on the
                    gobble-down.

Here

Where these islands lie
the quality of transience prevails
down all the aisles
and avenues
of the dispassionate air;

And the sea moves
through moon-pull,
enhancing the reality
of ancient certainties—
sliding with splash and glisten
along the ebb and flow of tide,

While the gluttonous cormorant flies,
in his 'appointed time',
at the apogee
of the clear eye's reach—
silent as a scream
in mind's remembering.

Like the fragile,
green-striped lizard, who pauses
mid-flight through hot sand
to look behind and stare,
and freezes there,
I'm staying. But I'm staying

By the cool employment
of my own volition, receiving
the old familiars of sun and moon

as easily as pools of casual water
standing in the forest after rain
receive the girth of pines;

And balancing the sense
of transience (nicely as pinions
of the hawk on thermals
rising from the sea) to take dominion
over all the deeps of mind.

Heading Out

gulls
racing
close over wake

stroke
cushions of air
under bellies

coast

take it again from one.

This Sea (Early)

Sheer air
sustained the carousel

while Sol
hurled a curve
across the far end of the beach

and zoomed
into diminishment by sky,
where forty pelicans
circled winnowing
in echelons of five, all but
brushing waves
with tips of wings.

Fish glinted
deep in seaswell.

This Sea (Late)

Had the Sea of Galilee
been as calm
as this one is now,
when Christ is said
to have walked on it,
Peter would not have been afraid.

This sea
lies flat, like oil lying
low in a basin,
and the horizon swings
deep indigo
against a transparent sky
with no clouds—
only birds;

miles out,
an occasional one
flashing between the fringed edges
of the incredulous eye,
tumbles and turns,
caught in a shaft
of lowering sun on wings.

There is nothing else
here
but the pellucid air
and the size of this calm—
almost,
but not quite,
solid enough to walk on.

*Some Incidental Intelligence
About the Pleasures Known to Fishermen
And to Fisherwomen*

"Atte the leese his holsom walke, and mery at his ease, a swete ayre of the swete savoure of the meede floures that makyth him hungry; he hereth the melodyous armony of fowles; he seethe the yong swannes, heerons, duckes, cottes, and many other foules, wyth their brodes; whyches, me semyth better than alle the noyse of houndys, the blastes of horneys, and the cryes of foulis, that hunters, fawkeners, and foulers can make. And if the anglers take fysshe, surely then there is no man merrier than he is in his spyrte."

—From *The Treatise of Fyssing with an Angle*, written by Dame Julianna Barnes, Prioress of the Nunnery of Sopewell, near St. Alban's, and part of a book known as *The Book of St. Albans*—Enprinted at Westmere by Wynkyn DeWorde, in 1496: Reprinted in John Major's introductory essay to *The Complete Angler, or, the Contemplative Man's Recreation* by Izaak Walton and Charles Cotton, edited by John Major, New York, 1844.

A Sometime Thing

You can talk
all you want to
about fishing—in a given place,
for instance, and whether
it is good
or bad there,
and about the virtues
of different kinds of bait.

The variations of tackle
to be had fill books,
and have a musical ring and rhythm,
to wit: 'A Shakespeare Spinning Gear,
with an eight-pound-test line (monofilament)
and a lead-headed, buck-tail jig.'

But, by and large,
no matter what,
fishing is a sometime thing:
One can be shut out—
especially in the surf.
The devotees don't care.
Fishing gives them an excuse
for simply being there—as owning
a dog can justify
walking in a city park, in beat-up
old shoes, at all kinds
of odd hours.

For example: this morning at dawn
there were twenty three trawlers

spread wide under a gray squall-line,
and wallowing
in a pewter sea.

When I cast my last bait
the birds and the boats had gone.
And the sea lapped green,
where I had followed it,
wading,
all the way out to the first sand-bar.

*When I recognized her butler's blond
side-whiskers nearing me round the bend
of the street—her butler, who talked to
her, who saw her lunching, as might one of
her friends—my heart stopped yet again,
as if I had been in love with him too.*

—*Marcel Proust.* Contre Sainte Beauve—The Countess.
Translated by Sylvia Townsend Warner

Daytime Moon Overhead

When you come rushing,
lunging through the passive air
into my ken
the thrum and hammer and boil
of me could be heard anywhere
within a sizeable area;

and I feel the color of soul (un-
controllable)
flow into my eyes
like the green on the back
of the sea
at this high tide.

Having lost my dark glasses
I try to hide
by wagging my tongue
in spurious complaint

hoping the shine in my eyes
will pass for anger.

After the Quarrel

To hear dolphins singing one
to another would not have been
less likely than the soft ocean,
smooth as cream pudding, we swam
this afternoon to lie cradled
in calm at a blue edge of sky.

Lightly we felt the lift and swing
of the primordial swell—gentle
as dolphin-song must be when dolphins
chasing golden pompano
swim to nose the eel-cool shallows
shimmering in the shadow of the wind.

But now,
down deeps of green
our dolphins swim the reaches of
their sonar. Fast. Silent as moon-set.

Hermit Crab

Any of numerous decapod Crustaceans of the families Paguridae *and* Parapaguridae, *having the body somewhat elongated, and the abdomen soft and more or less asymmetrical. They occupy the empty shells of Gastropods, and when owing to the growth of the crab, a shell becomes too small, they seek a larger one.*

—*Webster's New International Dictionary*

When the House Pinches

Consider now
the Hermit Crab, and how
he dwells—cozily rent-free—in
other creature's cast-off shells.
When they become too small,
he, cavalierly, scouts about

the sanded pastures of the sea
until he spots another house.
He always
finds a vacancy—inside
the empty mansion of a conch,
or other kind of Gastropod.

As plentiful as winkles
are his digs. And big enough.

But odd.

The Fifty Dogs of Bimini

are not the kind
to be afraid of
on the street

or anywhere else
for that matter—
undernourished curs

lying in the gutters
like cast-off beige
bath mats.

But, when the big cruisers
purl in from Lauderdale
and their pure-bred dogs

poodles
taffy-coloured cockers
Weimaraners   et cetera

come ashore
to run,
briefly unleashed,

the mongrels
leap from apathy
and all but tear them to pieces.

Doldrums

Today the air shoved a pile
of clouds down and down, until
parallel with the horizon,
weighing their light sky-kedges

one by one

they moved like sailing ships,
including two hermaphrodite brigs,
around the whole afternoon
along the green rim of the sea

and never fell off the edge.

But, slipping dizzy off and on,
my freaked out, rapid-transit mind,
alternately squealed and groaned
the long curve of the calm.

Voyage to Nowhere

Waving my hemstitched
Irish-linen cliché
across the widening river-slick
I watched you
waving circles with your new Harris-tweed
cap, handwoven in the Outer Hebrides.

As the ship began to shudder
to the long thrust of her shaft—
her backwash moiling briefly the thick legs
of the pier—beneath a mewl of gulls
and ribboned paper streaming—
I could still make out the colors in your tie;

When they blurred
to grey, I (instead of fainting)
wobbled below to my immaculate cabin
with your green cimbidiums trembling on
the dresser and the plastic hangers swinging
and clicking, empty, in the armoire.

Here, finding
that I could not last the peculiarly
hushed immediacy of being torn in two,

I died.

But for chaste love the Mulleth hath no peer;
For, if the fisher hath surprised her pheer,
As mad with woe, to shore she followeth,
Prest to consort him both in life and death,

—*Du Bartas, 1544-90*

School of Mullet

Maybe as many
as a hundred
by the footbridge
under morning light

a depth of fishes
turning
with a flick
the whole school

quick
and simultaneous
moving
as one fish.

I thought they had
black backs
until I saw
that each one carried

shadow
like a saddle
of the brother   swimming

over him.

Birdwatcher's Winter Beach

Roaming the late afternoon,
with binoculars,
he spotted a pair
of American goldeneye   among
a raft of scoter, scaup and loon,
swinging slowly through calm—
nearer shore, and then away,
under a light wind.

Zeroing in,
he caught the gleam
of the drake's
eye;   and held it
until a groundswell hove
the whole float of birds
away from him,   toward sky.

Gone ducks.

But, as he looked up,
three ring-billed gulls flew by

On the returning heave of dusk.

Night Swim in September

There was no moon.

The sea crashed black—
immensely roaring—
rolling in unseen
to slap us
where we stood thigh-deep
to meet it

and shivered in the cosmic light
of the three stars
we watched falling.

Our bodies
smiled their inward smiles
and needed warming. We turned

and ran across a field of shells,
white towels flapping,
back through the dunes
down thin planks slapping lightly
over sucking tongues of tide.

And while we ran
another summer died; but not
the one which hummed in us.

Crab's Path

I'd only climbed up to the top of the dunes,
when, turning to look
where the house should have loomed,
I saw it had slipped from my sight—into,
or under, the fog.

And I'd lost the sun
and the daytime moon. And I moved,
blind, down a path
as oblique as a crab's.

The thud of my heels on the sand
rose up through the tree
of my bones, by-passing the usual
channels of ear,
as though by an inner telegraphy—
and shook in my skull until it was full
of the bone's small commotions,
and I stood with both feet
in an unseen ocean.

Then my eyes found the curl
of low waves folding, slick and easy
as porpoises rolling. And I found in my ears
in the usual way (and instead
of the thud of my heels),

The hiss, whisper-thin, of that slate-grey sea.

But, I'd lost the fine sense of my own bone's tree.

Which

swim

      do you want

to be in

      even

a dead fish

can move

      with the stream

II. The Arrogant Flower

Beside the Castalia Fountain

Holy
is morning
to the lark,
as is night
to the winnowing owl.

Soul,
playing
In and Out the Window,
comes and goes
while a man sleeps.

On wings of lark?

And
in owl's beak?

Mischief

Sometimes
young crows engage
in a singular dialogue—

Uh-uh   Uh-uh   Uh-uh

it comes and goes
from high pines
across the cool
verandas of the mind

where grey doves
of the past roost among
the dust motes
in the cupola.

Rocking
on wind, the crows insinuate.

The doves stir: and complain.

The weathervane vacillates.

Where the Tree Grows Green

Snake and flower work together
In ancient patterning,
Scale enhancing petal,
Petal, scale,
In old affinities of style.

Blossoms blowing, any garden thrives,
Where there is room
To keep these two
Combined, with space enough
For each to move

In its own rhythm, separately.
The tree grows green
Toward sky. Fruit appears
And gleams, ready
on low branches, near

Both hand and eye—flourishing
Between the moist domains
Of two kinds of truth—
Where the snake crawls,
And the flower hides the root.

Sticks and Stones are Feathers

compared
with what hit the terrier,
digging in the herbaceous border
to bury a bone.

A man yelled a rock.
An old dog
         slunk home.

The Community of Snakes

Where do snakes go
When the bulldozers come
With shove and growl,
Pushing down the forest and the vine? Some,

If not most men, don't mind,
Nor care about the comings and the goings
Of the serpent. And would
Prefer to see the end of him—knowing

Nothing of where snakes go
When their woods fall down,
And the earth shakes
And gapes. And the structure of the air around

Fragments into shuddering sound.
But the community of snakes
Crawls along the ground,
Silent, through leaf and long grass, to escape;

Pushing further back to hide
In ever deeper forest. So, moved by fear,
The snakes will be—crawling
Ahead—The first to cross the last frontier.

What then?
Faced by such numbers of them,
Where will men
              Go?

I used to like to hear him admire the beauty of a flower it was a kind of gratitude for the flower itself; and a personal love for its delicate form and color. I seem to remember him gently touching a flower he delighted in; it was a simple admiration that a child might have.

—Sir Francis Darwin, writing about his father

The Clearest Image

My father has been dead now seven years;
and yet, the clearest image that I have
of him goes back (like a long-stored rug
unrolling quick with weight) to the day
I played, singing and alone, beneath
the Jersey pines, beside
ground-cover of arbutus through which
a great blacksnake had slid, silent
as butter melting, to hide in deeper shade.

Looking up,
I saw my father standing in a shaft of sun.

His watch-chain shone and glittered
like minnows I have seen, swimming and
flicking through shallows of a stream.
His tan shoes commandeered the sand.
He towered in his city suit above that hot,
green glade, his head inclining toward the
spray of pink arbutus trailing at our feet.

Then, as he turned to look at me, his
wonder shining light and shadow down,
I first knew myself to *be*—and

Unfolding like the flowers all around.

When I Consider the Beneficence of Unpolluted Air

On being born
I clove this ambience of air,
surmounted by the fleece
and witnessing of clouds;

Now, lightly it surrounds
me as I sleep,
like an invisible sheet,
and sweet I find the breathing
in and out of it (which all things
cleave in passing,
and which my square-nosed box
will butt when I go back to dust).

Borning again,
I would not choose to cleave
with wing, or fin, or tongue,
or the filamented laser-beams
of some, so far unknown
non-people people,
an airless atmosphere.

And yet, I surfaced
from the womb—swinging wildly
out of that buoyant encompassment
like a rowdy wedding bell;
and made it all the way to here.

And to the, then simple, beneficence of air.

The Sense of an Alien Presence

The sense of an alien presence intervenes
at the beginning of all kinds
of performances,
such as bumping a bee at the lip
of a flower, or meeting with a pair
of unexpecting eyes—an animal's,
or those of a child encountered
bent beside a keyhole.

All motion stops in such a confrontation;
a waiting happens,
however brief, of an enormous size,
with fine elaborations
of withdrawal and unfolding,
before the alien sense is rearranged—
and the eyes meet openly;

Or one can reach to set a flower,
trembling on its stem, into equilibrium.

The Cold Sky

We had the cold sky through the day,
around us everywhere.
And one great once it cried with geese;
there must have been
at least five thousand of them there—
grouping, wheeling, banking, with
their rusty gate-hinge talking, as they
dropped and plopped, wings down, onto the pond,
and rock-hard field beyond.

The moon rose massive, orange as fire.
But, when we saw it mirrored
high and pale,
on rivers twisting, frozen stiff
as death among the woods,
we shrugged down in our coats,
deep as we could—chilled to remembering
by rivers turned to steel,
that hate and fear, and being lost, are real.

Lines to a Young Ballerina

When,
in your tutu,
you surmount
a vertical
column
of air

to hover,
sustained
by your own
perfectly executed
entrechat,

birds
gliding down the wind,
jealous
of their supremacy,
will turn their heads
to look in,

while the stars
love you
because you have
become
one of them .

The Last Visit

Beside the Norway maple, behind
The brown stone wall where ivy climbed
Above the life of the street and the pneumatic
Sighs of buses passing, and children shouting
Their way to school as they did on every other day,
The neighborhood doctor died.
The line his grieving patients made ran two
Full blocks—right up to the church-yard wall.
Out of love, to see his face again, they came
With hope of drawing comfort from good-bye.

"He pulled my sons into their lives with those
Big hands of his." an aging mother said,
Remembering the five times joy.
The piano teacher thought—silent—
As she had kept the anguish of her years,
"He knew about the love I lost
And what it did to me."
The pharmacist smiled, and said: "He always
Had a brand new joke. And the way he worked
Those beagles of his through an open field
With that game leg he dragged home from
Anzio was something to ponder on."

Four decades back into the
Birth-blood of the town the talking flowed.
It made their old friend seem so real
He all but stood there with them on the street.
So they were unprepared,
Somehow defeated, at the end,

When they shuffled into the flower-filled room,
With tight-clenched hands and indrawn breath,
To find him lying, unaware and still,
Already diminished into memory
Beneath the towered silence of his death.

Poetry, as every poet knows, cannot be taught—that is, in the sense that a pure craft or trade can be taught. Nor can a 'would-be' poet be taught to become one. He must first 'be', as in the very beginning of his being he just 'is'. He is of the breed born, as one is born with brown eyes, or short fingers. What he makes of it—if, indeed, anything—depends on him as well as the favor of all the Gods and Muses; and unpoetic attributes such as physical endurance, adequate income and proper food. In addition (and perhaps most importantly) he needs a thick skin against those barbs which will dig into it—deeply; and from all kinds of unexpected directions.

The Papal Audience

We listened forty
minutes and
a young girl
fainted

before
the Holy Father
was born out
above the heads

of all
that crowd   his
white robes
gleaming

over a sea
of hands reaching
oh
Mamma Mia

breathed
the old woman
next to us   and
he was gone

*As we bounced
in our landrover onto the great
Serengeti Plains, where animals
flourish with the profusion of flowers,
the silhouettes of galloping zebra
and wildebeeste flowed the horizon
like a great tidal river at its high.*

—At Serengeti National Park
East Africa, February 1970

The Interior

Sometimes
seeking sleep,
instead of counting sheep,
I journey mind's country
deep into the interior

frequently coming upon
prides of gold-eyed lions
lounging savannah grasses
whose numberless
blades swish green sighs
sliced from wind leaning lightly
into the date-palm and yellow fever trees.

And I watch
the sacred ibises following their
decurved beaks through papyrus;
or, I stare ruins
of the dew-jewelled pool
where a spider fished his web all night,
running down the monofilaments
of his own silk
to pounce the moth—shaking
silver, wing-powder
down dreams
of mosquito-hawk, gadfly and gnat.

But, when
deep from the podocarpus forest,
scattering their nit-picking egrets
and opportunist baboons,

the elephants stampede—
hooves swinging under improbable knees,
ears flapping like gargantuan cabbage leaves—
to trumpet their vertical squeals (with
that wild blatt bulging the middle)
I freeze,

And my own dingles
fill up with Mustangs and Toyotas.
And biodegradable Godheads. And needles.

My mask fits as close as the skin on my teeth.

Two Songs

1

Come! The moonlight
lies in a pool of love
on the lap of
         the valley.

2

The autumn sun hangs in the sky,
Gentle as the grape upon the vine,
Giving a flavor to high noon
As sweet as grapes pressed into wine;

It pours full on the browning fields
To touch the very heart of stones.
And lingers on the pavement stoops
Where old men sit to warm their bones.

But, seeing amber on the leaves,
O how I wish that love could be
Wrapped against the tawniness—blossom,
Branch and root, like a delicate tree .

On Having Arrived at the Timber Line

So far,
we're just bumming around
looking up at the trees;
and I'm all uptight
for no reason more explicable
than the prospect
of identifying Betelgeuse again,*
remembering how—
especially when there is no moon—
stars *are*.

But, pragmatically speaking,
only Heaven knows
what has been going on
out there while we climbed two days
away from the news.   The ruby
could have come unpinned
from the shoulder
of Orion's lionskin—and slipped
to drift and disappear
among the ghosts

                of other

                    lost

                      familiars.

*Betelgeuse: A variable red giant star of the first magnitude—known as "The Ruby" on the shoulder of Orion's lionskin (the constellation Orion, that is)

Harsanyi

Immersed
in the disciplines
of the Liadov folksongs

he has obviously forgotten
all inner litanies
of subjective melancholy.

La! When he brings down
the baton his jowls
bounce and quiver.

Light refracted from the horns
shimmers his rimless glasses.
The bottoms of his blackbird

coattails lift. And
under Red Square
the old dust stirs.

The gypsies make camp
where the bearded barley
leans against the poppy.

The trained bear lumbers into dance.

A man cannot say, "I will compose poetry." The greatest poet ever cannot say it; for the mind in creation is as a fading coal, which some invisible influence, like an inconstant wind, awakens to transitory brightness; this power arises from within, like the color of a flower which fades and changes as it is developed. Could this influence be durable in its original purity and force, it is possible to predict the greatness of the results; but when composition begins, inspiration is already on the decline, and the most glorious poetry that has ever been communicated to the world is probably a feeble shadow of the original conceptions of the poet.

—*Percy Bysshe Shelley.* A Defense of Poetry

Pas de Trois

After she died

he moved among a mustering
of silences. Some,
large as sky,
towered like late-summer cumulous,
layer on layer, endless as prayer.
Others moved along
through windless aisles of space,
small as the involuntary
sighs of outworn patience;

only the grief
which soared among them
gave the lie
to utter nothingness.

Grief stooped. And lighted—
raven-hearted. Yellow-eyed—
leaning
from the dryest branch of all
his thought.

He leapt his shaken roots,
and hooded grief
with false indifference.

The silences,
inert as dust, drifted down.

Hidden Image

you sidled
into shadow
like a drug pusher
on the lam

I know you're there
somewhere   hiding
behind a word
most likely
SPEED? (you got away
fast enough)

but *lie low sheepie*
I know the waiting game
I'll be here
when you come out
and then I'll frisk you

my father
before he went on the nod
could whistle
on his fingers
high

      and wide enough

to crack the
        sky

Early Breakfast

When the cat

padded
across the lawn
his kill was almost

more
than he could carry
in his mouth—a big

grey squirrel

dangling
like a thick, wet-mop
dragging the ground
through snow

and the cat
like a fat black shadow
only closer than a shadow

and on quick feet.

The Earth does not Always Move Twice Under the Same Body During the Same Life

Run

the jig is up

betrayed by the entire
company of your hair
dancing wits-end
of love   in the light

leaping

from your psyche   like
a great rise of birds
meeting morning

Run

Run for it

The Ramblers

Nobody knows who planted those pink roses
Down along the railroad track, nor how long
Ago (except that it was at least four wars back).
They ramble down the bank beside the rails
Like a crowd of teen-age girls, who, leaving
Sunday School to go home by the woods,
Have mussed up their best dresses, roaming so.

The roses have tenacity. Their pink endures.
They were, I suppose, in a dooryard garden
When there were trees along that then country
Street, and a coal stove in the kitchen,
And Wednesday was the night for Missionary Meeting.
Pink Roses. One whole generation leaps
To life, all of a piece, flickering wanly

In my mind, like an old-time movie, when I
Ride that train. Click and clack along the track
It goes. I see the roses and remember
The grape-arbor out back, home-made lemonade,
And old folks on the front porch, sitting straight
In Creaking wicker chairs—talk, talk, talking
About Lincoln   damning John Wilkes Booth.

Above the Monarch's Wing

Dreaming our daytime dreams
we soon outrun the fractious mares of night;
and see blue air above the monarch's wing.
Rolling at fifty fathoms, passing stygian
grottoes, great herds of blue whale sing.

Looking out and looking in,
we roam the unfenced pastures of the mind—
the light around our bodies reflecting
our reflections.   Languidly, the anthered
Leopard Lily sways beneath the Sweet Bay Tree.

Dreaming the waking dream
we flow into dream's meaning. The stars go
swinging orderly through the vast aisles
of space. And in the seas numberless fishes
swim, unseen, toward the nets of fishermen.

Let all the birds and grasses celebrate.

*The Swallow
Turns a somersault;
   What has it forgotten?*

—*Otsuyu*

*Ah! Somersaulting
Swallow—You have forgotten
Just which end was up!*

Over the Bounding May

'Where are you?' you call,
from the dark of the porch—

'I'm out here, near the owl
who just spooked past my head
to a branch of the oak,
and with an eddy of bats
squeaking close (through incredibly
small animations
of air) to my ears.

'There's a fine surge of wind
in the elms,
and I'm seeing the house
from the garden-side in—
throwing its lights
on the white of the clapboards,
it looks like a ship under way;

'I have jumped it. The orchard
hangs close off the bow,
like a low-lying cloud,
where a sickle-moon nicks at the sky.
There's a towering wave
of the smell of May;
and I'm riding it high.'

Prelude

A certain kind of love
is like a new and striped snake;
perhaps he should be killed
and left to wriggle

where the sun
batters the gravel of the path
until night comes.

But, on the other hand,
suppose that he be innocent
of harm,
as well as beautiful—

and dead then?

Autumn Marsh: Updated

The gallinules among the lily-pads, slipped
out of eye's reach and into the reeds,
heads pumping ahead of their invisible feet,
as quickly as dreams from the near edge of sleep.

And I stood in the posture of wonder,
while the elaborations of the anhinga's wings,
stretched out behind a clump of sedge to catch
the sun, asserted the bird in passive space
like a stabile of unbuffed aluminum, commanding
a ramp at the Guggenheim as the consummate
water-turkey—dynamic among the abstractions.

A float of coots squawked and spooked,
breaking mirror of marsh into fountains of drops
splashing back splatter and sparkle.

The anhinga shook his wings and rose,
flapping to climb, legs trailing behind—high,
higher, higher—leading his shadow through
meadows of golden-rod, through celebrations
of grasses tasselling luminous air.

And silence flowed down his deliberate wake
to the autumn marsh at noon—round as moon,
or owl's eye. Or any other eye,
where love or terror lies mirrored.

Promptly,
like an army of mercenaries,

moving in to occupy, the awful regurgitations
of dredges on the far side of the refuge
assaulted the air.

Luminosities trembled.   Daymares
invaded my mind,
where a deputation of alligators sought counsel.

Looking Alive at Jacob's Pillow

Blink!

That hummingbird
might take your
eyes
for parts

of the

delphinium.

Son

When she first held him

his breath sweet
as the new grass   his chin
bobbing on her shoulder
with immaculate slobber

a current spiralled
the barriers of skin
between them

festooning
the innocent air
with infinite waggings
of beginning   and

electric as love's touch

the immutable pull
of shared blood

swirling Hosannah

High Hosannah

Treading the Gentle Water

I rolled so slowly, swimming
on my side, that when
I raised my stroking arm
the water hung on it
and caught the sun—stretching
like molten glass
when ready for the blowing.

I swam so—easy in the cradle
of the water,
where heads of roses drooped
against the cypress of the fence ,
for fifty lengths before I quit.
As I figured it,
had I put them end to end,
I would have made it through
the pasture (purple with furled
vetch) and all the way
to the half mile of post and rail
which marked the far boundary.

Later, dozing in a slant of sun,
I dreamt. And dreaming,
had a flowing feeling as I swam
slowly along this green,
projected line,
until I'd swum upon the sight
of one white stallion
and a chestnut mare. Side by side,
bellies deep in grass, they ran,

their tails stretched out
against the summer of the sky.

Gently treading gentle water,
then, I watched them
run until the stallion reared
and screamed. *Glass broke.*
Someone had dropped a bottle
on the flagstones.   I woke;
and missed the meeting
of the nightmare with the dream.
But all that night in my deep sleep
I had a flowing feeling left
from rolling slow and easy
through the meadows in between.

The X-Ray

As I stared at my luminous bones
I saw my own head rising
From the stem of my neck
To achieve an imperious balance,
Dominating the ordered progression
Of the vertrebrae—crowning
Their ineffable curve
Like an arrogant flower.   Blank,

In the shadowed profile, one eye-socket
Belied the presence of a living eye.
Blade-thin, the tip of the nose clove,
Like a miniature jib, intimate space
Above the teeth, while they,
Their chewing surfaces meeting nicely,
Showed grinding machines rising from beds
Of bone above jaw's low-hung cradle.

And I saw my meticulously sutured
Cranium—fortress and retainer of the mind—
Mutely affirming the inviolability
Of its chambered thoughts, hived
As an infinitude of bees,
Which when my skull begins turning
To slow stone will quicken, sempiternal,
In that holy continuum where consciousness
Burgeons and blooms, whenever a heart
First beats within a stilly womb.

Then, radiant, under a hover
Of angels drifting slowly down,

I glimpsed the whole round river of time—
'Until a time, and times,
And the dividing of time'—where I
Stood weeping awe's tears—again and again,
And yet again, and again, and again—at Olduvai,
And Knossus   And Ephesus   And Delphi—

Hurrahing the arrogant flower,
Divining the silent assertion of bones.

Selah.

*This book
was set in Garamond type
by A & B Typesetters, Concord, N.H.,
printed on 70 lb. Finch Opaque paper at
the Transcript Printing Co., Peterborough, N.H.
and bound by the General Book Binding Co.,
South Hadley, Mass.*